# M First Pocket Guide

# FLORIDA

## By Carole Marsh

FLORIDA
Experience

# The GALLOPADE GANG

Carole Marsh
Bob Longmeyer
Michele Yother
Michael Marsh
Sherry Moss
Chad Beard
Sue Gentzke
Cecil Anderson

Steven Saint-Laurent
Deborah Sims
Andrew Brim
Andrea Detro
John Raines
Karin Petersen
Billie Walburn
Doug Boston

Kim Holst
Jennifer McGann
Ellen Miller
William Nesbitt, Jr.
Kathy Zimmer
Wanda Coats

Published by
GALLOPADE INTERNATIONAL

www.floridaexperience.com
800-536-2GET • www.gallopade.com

Gallopade is proud to be a member of these educational organizations and associations:

**NSSEA**

**ASCD**

SHOP A MEMBER
School, Home, & Office Products Association

## Other Florida Experience Products

• The Florida Experience!
• The BIG Florida Reproducible Activity Book
• The Fabulous Florida Coloring Book
• My First Book About Florida!
• Florida "Jography": A Fun Run Through Our State
• Florida Jeopardy!: Answers and Questions About Our State
• The Florida Experience! Sticker Pack
• The Florida Experience! Poster/Map
• Discover Florida CD-ROM
• Florida "Geo" Bingo Game
• Florida "Histo" Bingo Game

A Word From the Author... (okay, a few words)...

Hi!

Here's your own handy pocket guide about the great state of Florida! It really will fit in a pocket—I tested it. And it really will be useful when you want to know a fact you forgot, to bone up for a test, or when your teacher says, "I wonder . . ." and you have the answer—instantly! Wow, I'm impressed!

Get smart, have fun!

*Carole Marsh*

**Florida Basics**

**Florida Geography**

**Florida History**

**Florida People**

**Florida Places**

**Florida Nature**

**Florida Miscellany**

Florida Basics explores your state's symbols and their special meanings!

Florida Geography digs up the what's where in your state!

Florida History is like traveling through time to some of your state's great moments!

Florida People introduces you to famous personalities and your next-door neighbors!

Florida Places shows you where you might enjoy your next family vacation!

Florida Nature - no preservatives here, just what Mother Nature gave to Florida!

All the real fun stuff that we just HAD to save for its own section!

## Who Named You?

Florida's official state name is...

# Florida

**Word Definition**

OFFICIAL: appointed, authorized, or approved by a government or organization

Florida is one of the states to be on a year-2004 commemorative quarter! Look for it in cash registers everywhere!

### Statehood:
### March 3, 1845

Florida was the 27th state to ratify the U.S. Constitution.

Coccinella Noemnotata is my name!

4

## Latin Flavor

Spanish explorer Juan Ponce de León named *Florida* in April 1513. He arrived in Florida during the Spanish Feast of Flowers, *Pascua Florida* (Flowery Easter). Some say he named Florida for the abundance of flowers he saw there. For many years, Spain used the name to refer to the entire Atlantic Coastline from Florida to Newfoundland, Canada.

Years ago the Spanish would say, "La Florida."

# What's In A Name?

"Florida" is not the only name by which Florida is recognized. Like many other states, Florida has a nickname.

**State Nickname**

The Sunshine State

Florida made the *Guinness Book of World Records* for the most consecutive days of sunshine.

Wooow! You learn something new everyday.

## State Capital:
# Tallahassee

Established as state capital on March 4, 1824

State Capital & Capitol

The Creek origin for Tallahassee means "old friend" or "old town."

Word Definition

CAPITAL: a town or city that is the official seat of government
CAPITOL: the building in which the government officials meet

# Who's in Charge Here?

Florida's GOVERNMENT has three branches:

LEGISLATIVE     EXECUTIVE     JUDICIAL

**State Government**

*The legislative branch is called the General Assembly.*

TWO HOUSES: the Senate (40 members); House of Representatives (120 members)

A governor, lieutenant governor, and Cabinet

SUPREME COURT Seven Justices including one Chief Justice

The number of legislators is determined by population, which is counted in the census every ten years; the numbers above are certain to change as Florida grows and prospers!

When you are 18 and register according to Florida laws — you can vote! So please do! Your vote counts!

State Flag

Riddle:
What 5 flags
have flown over
Pensacola, Florida,
which is known
as the City of
Five Flags?

The State Flag
of Florida was
adopted in 1899.
It is always found
atop the state
capitol, and all
state, city, and
town buildings.

Answer: The flags of Spain, France, England, the Confederacy, and the United States.

# State Seal

State
Seal &
Motto

Features a brilliant sun, a Sabal Palm tree, a steamboat under sail, and a Seminole woman scattering flowers.

Word Definition

MOTTO: a sentence, phrase, or word expressing the spirits or purpose of an organization or group

# State Motto

## In God We Trust

The first proposed state motto was, "Let Us Alone!"

Where else is this phrase seen?

# State Bird

## Birds of A Feather

The state bird of Florida is the Mockingbird, *Mimus polyglottos,* known for its singing ability. It can also mimic other birds, even a dog's bark.

State
Bird

Mockingbirds are known for their defensive behavior of the family nest. They've even been known to chase off crows and cats!

State
Tree

# SABAL PALM

The Sabal Palm is a majestic tree and the most common tree in the state. It grows in almost any type of soil. It provided food and shelter for early settlers.

# ORANGE BLOSSOM

The state flower of Florida is found on orange trees.

Orange Blossom - *Citrus sinensis*

Orange trees start producing at 4 or 5 years of age and continue up to 50 years!

The orange blossom is one of the most fragrant flowers in Florida.

# Florida Panther

**State Animal**

A descendant of the mountain lion, the Florida panther is a large tan cat with a long, black-tipped tail and white on its belly. It grows to be 5-8 feet (1.5-2.5 meters) long! In 1982, Florida students voted the panther to be Florida's state animal.

The most endangered of all of Florida's animals is the panther. It has been protected from legal hunting in Florida since 1958.

**RIDDLE:** If the state flower got mixed up with the Florida Panther, what would you have?

ANSWER: An Orange Panther

"Conch" comes from the Greek word meaning "shell."

*—Pleuroploca gigantea—*

Also known as the giant band shell, the Horse Conch is native to marine waters around Florida and grows up to 24 inches (60 centimeters). It is the outside skeleton for a soft-bodied animal that lives inside it.

**State Shell, Stone, Gem**

Agatized coral is Florida's state stone. Coral reefs are the tropical forests of the sea. Without them, Florida's ecosystem would not survive.

Moonstone is a somewhat see-through, bluish mineral found worldwide. It is <u>not</u> from the Moon! Florida adopted the moonstone as the official State Gem in 1970, soon after Neil Armstrong and "Buzz" Aldrin landed on the Moon on July 20, 1969.

Sanibel Island has an official posture called "The Sanibel Stoop." It is derived from the stooped position taken by all the beachcombers picking up shells!

# State Beverage

## "O.J."

**State Beverage**

Florida produces about 40 billion oranges a year. If they were laid end to end, they could reach 2 million miles into space. That's like going to the Moon and back 4 times!

### Florida Orange Juice Smoothie

Blend together orange juice, strawberries, bananas, milk, and ice.

The Spanish introduced the first orange trees to Florida in 1570.

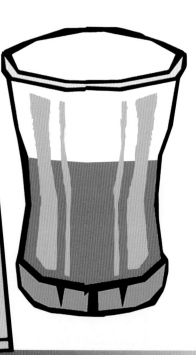

# State Mammals

The manatee is the state freshwater mammal. Also called sea cows, manatees are slow, gentle mammals that feed on water plants growing in coastal rivers and shallows. Manatees are distant cousins of the elephant.

*Manatees*

The state salt water mammal is the playful dolphin. They are often seen in bays and harbors. They send messages to each other by whistling and squealing. If one member is injured, the group will help it to the surface to breathe.

*Dolphin*

I think I see a manatee!

Florida has a county and a river called Manatee. It also appears on some automobile license plates.

# The Swanee River

State Song

Also known as "Old Folks at Home." Stephen C. Foster wrote the song in 1851. The spelling of the river is different in the song because he needed a river name with 2 syllables. The river in Florida is actually spelled Suwannee.

The original song by Stephen C. Foster was written in African-American dialect.

# Praying Mantis

**State Insect**

*Pleuroploca gigantea*

The praying mantis is cannibalistic. (They eat their own species.) The female will even eat her own mate!

Praying Mantises get their name from the way they fold their forelegs in front, ready to catch their victims. This position looks like they are "praying" - get it? They are mistaken for leafs or twigs even though they can grow to 3 inches (7.6 cm) long.

# Atlantic Sailfish

The sailfish gets its name from its large sail-shaped dorsal fin. They will fold their "sail" against their body to swim rapidly, up to 60 miles per hour (100 km per hour).

State Fish

Stuart is known as the sailfish capital of the world.

# Florida Bass

The state freshwater fish is the Florida bass or largemouth bass. The female can lay 25,000 eggs at one time and they hatch in just a few days.

Florida was an island millions of years ago, buried by rising sea levels and reappearing when the sea lowered.

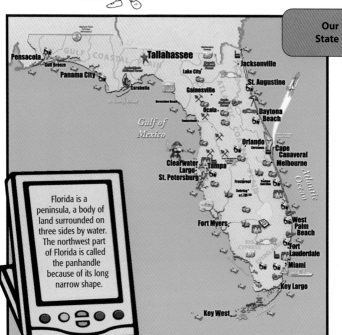

Florida is a peninsula, a body of land surrounded on three sides by water. The northwest part of Florida is called the panhandle because of its long narrow shape.

Florida is located in the southeastern corner of the U.S. Florida's peninsula extends between the Atlantic Ocean and the Gulf of Mexico.

**State Location**

Contiguous United States

Florida →

Word Definition

LATITUDE: Imaginary lines which run horizontally east and west around the globe
LONGITUDE: Imaginary lines which run vertically north and south around the globe

# State Neighbors

**These border Florida:**

**States:** Georgia
Alabama

**Bodies of water:** Atlantic Ocean
Gulf of Mexico
Straits of Florida

**State Neighbors**

In 1888, due to the frequency of shipwrecks along Florida's coast, the federal government built five houses of refuge where shipwreck survivors could seek shelter. Stuart is home to one of these houses.

# Exploring Florida

Florida is 160 miles (256 kilometers) east to west... or west to east. Its greatest distance along the panhandle is 361 miles (577.6 kilometers.)

**East–West**
**North–South**
**Area**

Florida is 447 miles (715 km) north to south... or south to north. Either way, it's still a long drive!

**Total Area: Approx. 59,928 square miles**
**Land Area: Approx. 53,937 square miles**

Florida has 1,300 miles (2,100 km) of coastline. That's a LOT of beaches!

Key West has the distinction of being the southernmost point in the continental United States. Be sure to get your picture taken with this world-famous buoy!

THE CONCH REPUBLIC

★ 90 Miles to Cuba

THE
SOUTHERNMOST
POINT
CONTINENTAL
U.S.A.
KEY WEST. FL.

# Highs & Lows

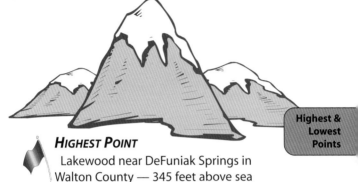

Highest & Lowest Points

### HIGHEST POINT

Lakewood near DeFuniak Springs in Walton County — 345 feet above sea level (105 meters)

> The Everglades National Park is 50 miles (80 km) wide and only 6 inches (15 cm) deep!

### LOWEST POINT
Sea Level — Along Florida's long coastline. *What could be lower than sea level? ...Florida's largest known sinkhole is 320 feet (97 meters) wide and 150 feet (46 meters) deep! In 1981 it caved in and swallowed 6 cars and a house!*

## I'm County-ing on You!

Florida is divided into 67 counties.

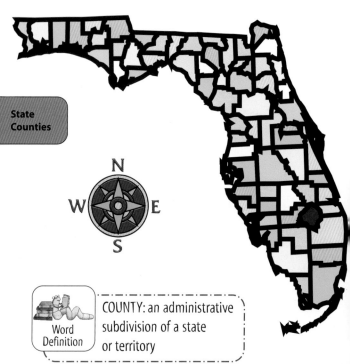

State
Counties

N
W E
S

Word
Definition

COUNTY: an administrative
subdivision of a state
or territory

# Natural Resources

***Forests*** make up almost half of Florida's land area.

Word Definition

NATURAL RESOURCES: things that exist in or are formed by nature

## *Minerals:*

- Phosphate
- Titanium
- Limestone
- Fuller's earth
- Mineral sands
- Brick clay
- Peat
- Pure silica sand
- Kaolin -
  a pottery clay
- Monazite
- Staurolite
- Rare earth
  concentrate
- Coquina rock

Almost all of the nation's frozen orange juice is from Florida!

Coquina rock, a type of limestone made from broken coral and sea shells, was a popular construction material in the early 1900s. Houses made of coquina can still be seen today.

27

## Weather, Or Not?!

Florida summers are hot, humid and long. Winters are mild with some cool winds from the north.

Key West has the highest average temperature in the country.

Highest temperature: 109°F (42°C), Monticello
June 29, 1931

°F=Degrees Fahrenheit °C=Degrees Celsius

Lowest temperature: -2°F (-18°C), Tallahassee
February 13, 1899

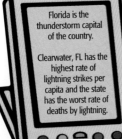

Florida is the thunderstorm capital of the country.

Clearwater, FL has the highest rate of lightning strikes per capita and the state has the worst rate of deaths by lightning.

## CLIMB EVERY MOUNTAIN

Florida's topography includes
six land areas:

**Tallahassee Hills**
**Central Highlands**
**Coastal Lowlands**
**Southern Lowlands**
**Western Highlands**
**Marianna Lowlands**

Most of Florida is made up of low
flatlands or Coastal Plains.

**Word Definition**

TOPOGRAPHY: the
detailed mapping of
the features of a
small area or district

Florida is known
for its many
sinkholes and
artesian springs.

The Florida
Sunken Gardens
started out as a
sinkhole.

Sea Level

100 m / 328 ft
200 m / 656 ft
500 m / 1,640 ft
1,000 m / 3,281 ft
2,000 m / 6,562 ft
5,000 m / 16,404 ft

Topography

# Rocky Top

### *"The" Mountain*

Florida's only mountain is located in central Florida and is 325 feet (99 meters) high.

**State Geography**

There is a "mountain" of oyster shells at the Canaveral Seashore called Turtle Mound that is 40 feet (12 meters) high. The shells are the Indian leftovers from 600 years of oyster dinners!

"On top of Old Smokey...."

## Row, Row, Row your boat...

Florida has basically 3 types of rivers:

Fort Lauderdale is known as the Venice of America because of its 185 miles (296 kilometers) of waterways.

**1. Blackwater** - the water looks black from organic acids from swamps and forests

**2. Alluvial** - muddy brown from the transport of sediment and upstream erosion of silt-clay

**3. Springfed** - mostly clear from springs

Major Rivers

- **Wakulla**
- **Choctawhatchee**
- **Kissimmee**
- **Withlacoochee**
- **Suwannee**
- **Escambia**
- **St. Johns**
  (Florida's longest and only north-flowing river)
- **Ochlockonee**
- **Peace**
- **Santa Fe**
- **Caloosahatchee**
- **St. Mary's**
- **Apalachicola**
- **Oklawaha**

Gone Fishin'

**Major Lakes**

Lake Okeechobee, Florida's largest lake, is about 700 square miles (1,813 sq km) but its average depth is only about 8 feet (2.4 meters).

- LAKE OKEECHOBEE
- APOPKA
- CRESCENT
- GEORGE
- HARRIS
- KISSIMMEE
- ORANGE
- TOHOPEKALIGA

The 1.5 mile (2.5 km) fishing pier in Pensacola is the longest in the world!

Word Definition

RESERVOIR: a body of water stored for public use

# THE COUNTRY MOUSE - THE CITY MOUSE

Have you heard these wonderful Florida city, town, and crossroad names? Perhaps you can start your own collection!

**Cities & Towns**

## LARGE CITIES:

Miami
St. Augustine
Tallahassee
Fort Lauderdale
St. Petersburg
Tampa
Orlando
Jacksonville
Hialeah

## OTHER TOWNS:

Mayo
Watertown
Bell
Citra
Mulberry
Venus
Jupiter
Neptune Beach
Indiantown
Opa Locka
Christmas
Niceville

# Transportation

### Major Interstate Highways
I-95, I-10, I-75,
Florida Turnpike
(Sunshine State Parkway)
Everglades Parkway
(Alligator Alley)
United States Highway 1
Highway A1A

### Railroads

Transportation

Steamboats gave way to railroads as the major form of transportation in the 1880s. In the early 1990s Florida had 2,874 miles (4,625 kilometers) of railroad track.

### Major Airports
Miami International
Orlando International
Tampa International
Fort Lauderdale

### Seaports
Miami
Tampa
Jacksonville
Port Canaveral
Port Everglades
Palm Beach

# Timeline

| | |
|---|---|
| 1513 | Spanish explorer Juan Ponce de León lands on Florida coast |
| 1565 | Pedro Menéndez de Avilés establishes St. Augustine |
| 1698 | Spanish settlement established in Pensacola |
| 1750 | Creek Indians migrate to Florida; become known as Seminole |
| 1822 | Florida becomes a U.S. territory |
| 1836 | Florida's first railroads begin operating |
| 1845 | Florida admitted to the Union as the 27th state |
| 1861 | Florida secedes from the Union and joins the Confederacy |
| 1926 | Mediterranean fruit fly infestation |
| 1928 | More than 1,800 killed in Okeechobee area hurricane |
| 1950 | Space research and rocket-testing center opens at Cape Canaveral |
| 1986 | Space shuttle *Challenger* explodes after launch from Cape Canaveral |
| 1992 | Hurricane Andrew hits southern Florida |

**State History Timeline**

—2001—
Into the 21st Century!

St. Augustine was named after a saint in 1565. It is the oldest city in the country and has the oldest documented national cemetery in the U.S.

Earliest migrations of humans to Florida is estimated at about 10,000 years ago!

# Here come the Europeans!

When the first Europeans arrived in Florida there were three major nations already living there. The Calusa, Timucua, and Apalachee were farmers and hunters and lived peacefully with the Spanish for nearly 200 years.

# Native Americans Once Ruled!

There were probably about 350,000 Native Americans when the first Spanish arrived in Florida in the 1500s. By the 1700s, the first people from Florida were gone. They had either died of diseases like measles, smallpox, and typhoid fever, or had been forced into slavery in Georgia or South Carolina.

Early Indians

Word Definition

WAMPUM: beads, pierced and strung used by Indians as money, or for ornaments or ceremonies.

37

# Land Ho!

Rumors of gold drew Juan Ponce de León to Florida. He tried to start a colony but was wounded in battle and went back to Cuba where he died. Another Spanish expedition led by Pánfilo de Narváez came to Florida to start a colony in 1528. They landed on what is now called Tampa Bay. They were in search of gold but didn't find any.

Exploration

Hernando de Soto discovered the Mississippi River.

Jean Ribault discovered the St. Johns River.

## Home, Sweet, Home

Spain was the first to colonize Florida. Many missions were established between Saint Augustine and Tallahassee. The first colony in

Florida was established in 1521. Juan Ponce de León brought colonists to the Gulf Coast somewhere near Charlotte Harbor. The first colony did not last, because of fighting with Native Americans.

**Colonization**

Century-old conch houses in Key West have a distinctive look from those anywhere else in the country, with big verandas, shutters, ornate railings, long eaves and gutters, and roof hatches called scuttles (to release heat.)

It is said that Ponce de León searched Florida for the mythical Fountain of Youth.

In the Keys, a native-born Key Wester is called a "conch."

# Not just for breakfast

Florida leads the country in producing citrus fruits—70% of the nation's total citrus fruit production. Oranges, grapefruits, tangerines, tangelos, limes, and lemons are all citrus fruits.

**Key Crop/ Product**

The Spanish brought citrus fruits to Florida in the 1700s.

# Fact or fiction?

● September 3, 1969, hundreds of golf balls fell out of the sky, pelting the town of Punta Gorda!

● December 5, 1945, five U.S. Navy bombers disappeared in the Bermuda Triangle after taking off from Ft. Lauderdale. The "flying boat" sent to find them also disappeared!

● November 1987-May 1988, Gulf Breeze: Ed Walters claimed that he was "repeatedly" abducted by a UFO. (Do you believe him?)

● Homesick sailors used to mistake manatee for mermaids. At a distance they thought their flippers looked like hands. (The Latin word *manaus* means "having hands").

● At the bottom of Spook Hill in Lake Wales, your car may travel uphill without the engine running!

Legends & Lore

## OF HUMAN BONDAGE

Early colonists enslaved Native Americans in Florida. Later, colonists enslaved Africans, and brought them to North America. Many of these Africans escaped and joined groups of Native Americans. This group of runaway slaves and Native Americans became known as the Seminole. The Creek term *simanóle* means "runaways," or "those who separate."

**Slaves and Slavery**

The issue of slavery and state's rights led to the Civil War. In 1863, the Emancipation Proclamation, issued by U.S. President Abraham Lincoln, freed the slaves in areas still under Confederate control.

# Revolution

# Freedom?

During the American Revolution, 13 colonies under British rule decided to revolt against the king and start their own country. However, some colonists in Florida remained loyal to the King of Great Britain. They were called loyalists. Loyalists from other colonies fled to Florida. After the revolution, many loyalists left Florida and settled in the West Indies, which were still held by Britain.

Revolution

In St. Augustine, the loyalists burned pictures of John Hancock and Samuel Adams who were heroes of the Revolutionary War.

## Brother

The Civil War was fought between the American states. The argument was over the right of the states to make their own decisions, including whether or not to own slaves. Some of the southern states began to secede (leave) the Union. In January of 1861, Florida became one of the first states to secede and form the Confederate States of America.

**The Civil War!**

Word Definition

RECONSTRUCTION: the recovery and rebuilding period following the Civil War.

# The Civil War!

## vs. Brother

There was only one major battle in Florida during the Civil War. In 1864, Union soldiers marched in to take over Tallahassee. They also wanted to recruit slaves, take cotton and lumber, and stop Florida from supplying the Confederates. They lost the battle and never tried to invade again.

More Americans were killed during the Civil War than during World Wars I and II!

# Get It In Writing!

Treaty of Paris
1763

U.S. Declaration of Independence
1776

U.S. Constitution-written 1787
effective 1789

Second Treaty of Paris
1783

Treaty of San Lorenzo
1795

Adams-Onis Treaty
1819

Florida's present constitution
1968

# Immigrants

## WELCOME TO AMERICA!

Floridians have come to Florida from other states and many other countries on almost every continent! As time has gone by, Florida's population has grown more diverse. This means that people of different races and from different cultures and ethnic backgrounds have moved to Florida.

**State Immigrants**

*In the past, many immigrants came to Florida from European countries. Slaves migrated (involuntarily) from Africa. More recently, people have migrated to Florida from Cuba and Haiti. Only a certain number of immigrants are allowed to move to America each year. Many of these immigrants eventually become U.S. citizens.*

# 1888

Typhoid Fever takes the
lives of thousands

# 1898

Severe frost in north Florida
forces citrus growers south

**Disasters &
Catastrophes**

# 1928

More than 1,800 killed in
Okeechobee area hurricane

# 1992

Hurricane Andrew hits
southern Florida

A category 5
hurricane is rated
as devastating,
with winds
reaching more
than 155 miles
per hour!

# 1998

Wildfires destroy
500,000 acres and
hundreds of buildings

# Legal Stuff

# 1889

Poll tax introduced and a state medical board is created

# 1937

Florida removes poll tax

# 1969

Florida schools integrated

# 1971

Florida's first income tax

# 1999

6-year-old Cuban refugee Elián González is rescued from the ocean. Following an international custody battle, he returns to Cuba in June, 2000.

# Women

## 1920

Women gained suffrage nationally through the 19th Amendment. Florida was the last state to ratify the amendment in 1969.

## 1933

Betty Skelton Frank became the first female inductee of the International Automotive Hall of Fame after breaking world record land speeds four times. She was also the first woman elected to the Aerobatic Hall of Fame in 1988.

## 1971

Women

In 1971, Jacqueline Cochran was inducted into the Aviation Hall of Fame. She received the Distinguished Service Medal and earned more speed, distance, and altitude records than any other pilot of her time. She also led the Women Air Force Service Pilots in World War II.

## 1978

Janet Reno became the state attorney in 1978, later becoming the first woman to be appointed as U.S. Attorney General.

## 1991

Carrie White was the world's oldest known person at age 116 when she died in 1991.

Word Definition

SUFFRAGE: the right or privilege of voting

# Fight!, Fight!, Fight!

Wars that Floridians participated in:

- French and Indian War
- Revolutionary War
- War of 1812
- First, Second, & Third Seminole Wars
- Civil War
- World War I
- World War II
- Korean War
- Vietnam War
- Persian Gulf War

Wars

# Disney's Dream

The biggest entertainment complex in the world is Walt Disney World in Orlando, Florida. It has four main theme parks - the Magic Kingdom, EPCOT Center, Animal Kingdom, and Disney-MGM Studios. Others include Universal Studios, Sea World, and Gatorland. There are now Disneyland theme parks in Europe and Japan. Walter Elias Disney opened the first theme park in Anaheim, California in 1955. Disney World in Orlando opened in 1971, dramatically affecting the economy of central Florida.

Claim to Fame

There is a 6 foot mouse named Mickey in Disney World!

Holy-roly-poly!

# Indian Tribes

➤ Calusa
➤ Apalachee
➤ Tequesta
➤ Timucua
➤ Tocobaga
➤ Ais

Today there are 4 Federal Indian Reservations in Florida. The major tribes or nations are Seminole, Miccosukee, and Cherokee.

The Seminole were a group of Native Americans and runaway slaves. The Creek term *simanóle* means "runaways," or "those who separate." There are about 1,500 Seminole who still live in Florida.

The city of Hypoluxo's name comes from the Seminole expression "water all around – no get out".

53

# Here, There, Everywhere!

PÁNFILO DE NARVAEZ explored Florida

JUAN PONCE DE LEÓN, first European in Florida

Explorers & Settlers

HERNANDO DE SOTO, explored Florida; first European to reach the Mississippi River

JEAN RIBAULT, discovered the St. Johns River

NORMAN THARGARD, Astronaut - explored the "final frontier"

**These men and women played especially important roles in the creation of our state.**

# Founding Fathers

RENE GOULAINE DE LAUDONNIERE — established Fort Caroline

MENENDEZ DE AVILES —established San Agustin (Saint Augustine)

WILLIAM D. MOSELEY — elected first governor of Florida

# Founding Mothers

MARY MCLEOD BETHUNE — famous educator who also served as special advisor to President Franklin D. Roosevelt on problems of minorities

State Founders

RUTH BRYAN OWEN — First congresswoman from the Deep South and first American woman diplomat

MARY MARTHA REID — nurse who cared for soldiers in the Civil War. The first chapter of the United States Daughters of the Confederacy was named after her.

SIDNEY POITIER, movie actor born in Miami who won an academy award for *Lilies of the Field*

A. PHILIP RANDOLPH, labor and civil-rights leader; founded Brotherhood of Sleeping Car Porters Union

MARY MCLEOD BETHUNE, teacher at mission schools in Florida 1895-1904 who started the Daytona Normal and Industrial Institute for Girls. It later merged with Cookman Institute and became Bethune-Cookman College. Bethune was also the director of the National Youth Administration's Division of Negro Affairs and the first president of the National Council of Negro Women.

Famous African-Americans

JAMES WELDON JOHNSON, poet, essayist, educator, journalist, songwriter, diplomat, and lawyer. He collaborated with his brother to write "Lift Every Voice and Sing," which the NAACP adopted as the Negro national anthem.

## DID SOMEONE SAY BOO!?

**THE FOLLOWING GHOSTS ARE SAID TO HAUNT VARIOUS PLACES IN THE STATE!**

**A ghost at historic Kenilworth Lodge**

**Phantom ship southwest of Cortez**

**Sea monsters in St. Johns River**

**Water monsters in Suwanee River**

Ghosts & Monsters

**Mound Key has had reports of UFOs and the Skunk Ape (Bigfoot)**

Ghosts are also called specters, spirits, spooks, poltergeists, banshees, and apparitions!

**ANTHONY CARTER**
football player

**DWIGHT GOODEN AND DON SUTTON**
baseball players

**BILL FRANCE, Jr.** founded NASCAR in Daytona Beach

**CHRIS EVERT LLOYD** tennis champion

Sports Figures

## TEAMS
Florida Marlins (Miami) - baseball
Tampa Bay Devil Rays - baseball
Tampa Bay Buccaneers - football
Jacksonville Jaguars - football
Miami Heat - basketball
Orlando Magic - basketball
Florida - (Miami) Panthers - hockey
Tampa Bay Lightning - hockey
Miami Dolphins - football

# Entertainers

* ★ "CANNONBALL" ADDERLEY, jazz musician

* ★ GLORIA ESTEFAN, Cuban-American songwriter and singer

* ★ TOM PETTY, singer, songwriter

* ★ LYNYRD SKYNYRD, musical group

* ★ SIDNEY POITIER, actor

* ★ JOHN & CHARLES RINGLING, circus owners

* ★ BEN VEREEN, actor

* ★ JIMMY BUFFETT, musician

* ★ BURT REYNOLDS, actor

* ★ FAYE DUNAWAY, actress

* ★ PAT BOONE, singer

* ★ FERNANDO BUJONES, ballet dancer

* ★ RAY CHARLES, musician, studied in St. Augustine

* ★ DEBBIE HARRY, Miami born singer, formerly of rock group Blondie

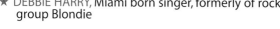

Entertainers

**RIDDLE:** Which musician founded the Manatee Protection League and initiated the Adopt-a-Manatee program?

ANSWER: Jimmy Buffett

# Authors

## PENS ARE MIGHTIER THAN SWORDS!

- ERNEST HEMINGWAY, author
- CARL HIAASEN, mystery novelist and columnist
- ZORA NEAL HURSTON, famous folklorist, novelist, and anthropologist
- JAMES WELDON JOHNSON, poet
- JOHN DANN MACDONALD, author
- SIDNEY LANIER, poet and author
- HARRIET BEECHER STOWE, author, best known for anti-slavery novel *Uncle Tom's Cabin*
- LOIS LENSKY, children's author and illustrator
- MARJORIE KINNAN RAWLINGS, author
- MACKINLAY KANTOR, author and correspondent who won Pulitzer Prize for *Andersonville*
- TENNESSEE WILLIAMS, author, had a home in Florida

*Florida: Its Scenery, Climate, and History* was written by Sidney Lanier.

**nom de plume:** French for pen name, a fictitious name a writer chooses to write under

**RIDDLE:** Who wrote the famous anti-slavery novel *Uncle Tom's Cabin*?

Answer: Harriet Beecher Stowe

# Artists & Architects

**JACQUES DE MORGUES LE MOYNE**, French artist and writer. First known artist to visit the U.S. on an expedition to Florida. His writing and drawings of the Timucuan Indians were the earliest exposure of Native American life to Europeans.

**JOHN JAMES AUDUBON**, artist, ornithologist. This famous naturalist-artist spent much time in the Keys of Florida. The Audubon Society is named in his honor.

**ADDISON MIZNER**, eccentric architect who built lavish mansions for wealthy people in the 1920s.

**FRANK LLOYD WRIGHT**, architect. Florida is one of the only places to see multiple buildings designed by him.

**WINSLOW HOMER**, artist who painted in Florida in the 19th century.

## EDUCATORS AND TEACHERS

**MARY MCLEOD BETHUNE**, founder Bethune-Cookman College

**ARCHIE F. CARR**, international authority and educator on reptiles; biologist and author.

**SAMUEL CHAPMAN ARMSTRONG**, founder of Hampton Normal & Industrial Institute

## DOCTORS AND SCIENTISTS

**THOMAS ALVA EDISON**, inventor most famous for the moving picture camera, the phonograph, and the incandescent electric light bulb

**JOHN GORRIE**, physician and inventor, first in the U.S. to patent a mechanical refrigeration machine

Educators & Scientists

**SAMUEL ALEXANDER MUDD**, physician unjustly convicted of treating John Wilkes Booth's broken leg. He was pardoned after treating inmates of yellow fever.

**MARSHALL W. NIRENBERG**, biochemist awarded Nobel Prize for his work in proteins and genetics

**BENJAMIN GREEN** developed the first suntan cream in 1944

**LUE GIM GONG** horticulturist who developed late-ripening, frost-resistant oranges

# Pirates & Soldiers

## Pirates

**JOHN GOMEZ**
Panther Key was renamed Gomez Key after "Old John" Gomez.

**BLACK CAESAR**, black pirate, who, for many years, hid out in the mangroves of Biscayne Bay but was eventually discovered and hung.

## Soldiers

**ANDREW JACKSON**, army general, military governor of Florida, seventh president of the U.S.

**JOSEPH W. STILWELL**, army general

**THOMAS SIDNEY JESSUP**, military leader

**CHARLES PELOT SUMMERALL**, army general

**EDMUND KIRBY-SMITH**, military officer

**ZACHARY TAYLOR**, military leader and twelfth president of the U.S.

**NAPOLEON BROWARD**, military leader and politician

**OSCEOLA**, celebrated Indian leader of 2nd Seminole War

Pirates & Soldiers

*Joseph Stilwell was nicknamed "Vinegar Joe" for his outspoken behavior.*

## GOOD GUYS

● In 1993, 103 year old Marjory Stoneman Douglas received the Medal of Freedom for her lifelong dedication to helping preserve the National Everglades.

● Julius Stone, Florida head of the Federal Emergency Relief Administration, set up the Key West Administration and recruited volunteers in the 1930s to restore Key West into a thriving community.

## BAD GUYS

● The Barker Gang, led by "Ma" Barker, also known as "Machine Gun Kate," had a secret hideout near Ocala. Their stay there ended in a 6 hour shootout on January 16, 1935.

● "Scarface" Al Capone established a home on Palm Island despite some efforts to boot him out of the state. After an 11-year jail sentence, he returned to Palm Island and remained there in isolation until his death. He laid the foundation for casino gambling on the beach, making Dade County the Las Vegas of the 1930s.

## A FEW OF FLORIDA'S GOVERNORS

- Jeb Bush, 1999–
- Lawton Chiles, 1991–1998
- Bob Martinez, 1987–1991
- Reubin Askew, 1971–1979
- Leroy Collins, 1955–1961
- David Scholtz, 1933–1937
- Sidney J. Catis, 1917–1921
- W.S. Jennings, 1901–1905
- David S. Walker, 1865–1868

In 1985 Xavier L. Suarez became the first Cuban-born person to be elected mayor of Miami.

Governors

## TERRITORIAL

- William DuVal, 1822–1834
- John H. Eaton, 1834–1835
- Richard K. Call, 1835–1840
- Robert R. Reid, 1840–1841
- Richard K. Call, 1841–1844
- John Branch, 1844–1845

# Keeping the Faith

**First Presbyterian Church of Tallahassee**—Governors, councillors, and other officials of colonial Florida worshipped here.

**Cathedral of Saint Augustine**—The parish of the Cathedral of Saint Augustine is the oldest Roman Catholic Parish in the U. S.

**Christ Church**—built in 1832, it is the oldest church in Florida and a national historic landmark.

## SCHOOLS

*Some of Florida's colleges and universities:*

- University of Florida, Gainesville, founded in 1853
- Florida State University, Tallahassee, founded in 1857
- University of South Florida, Tampa, founded in 1956
- Florida Agricultural and Mechanical University, Tallahassee, founded in 1887
- University of West Florida, Pensacola, founded in 1963
- Florida Atlantic University, Boca Raton, founded in 1961
- University of Central Florida, Orlando, founded in 1963
- University of North Florida, Jacksonville, founded in 1965
- Florida International University, Miami, founded in 1965

**Churches and Schools**

The oldest wooden schoolhouse in the U.S. still stands in St. Augustine. It was built in the 1500s.

# Lest We Forget

## Historic Sites

★ Dade Battlefield State Historic Site
★ San Marcos de Apalache State Historic Site
★ Olustee Battlefield State Historic Site
★ Fort Gadsen State Historic Site
★ Gamble Plantation State Historic Site
★ Kingsley Plantation State Historic Site
★ Koreshan State Historic Site
★ Crystal River State Archaeological Site
★ Yulee Sugar Mill State Historic Site

## Parks

★ Everglades National Park
★ Big Cypress National Preserve
★ Apalachicola National Forest
★ Osceola National Forest
★ Biscayne National Park

★ Dry Tortugas National Park
★ Ocala National Forest
★ Myakka River State Park
★ Wakulla Springs State Park

# Famous Residents

★ The Hemingway Home and Museum, in Key West, home of Ernest Hemingway

★ Ringling Museum and Home - home of John Ringling, in Sarasota, also named "Cá d'Zan," Venetian dialect for "House of John"

★ Edison and Ford Homes, in Ft. Meyers (Homes of Thomas Edison and Henry Ford are next door to each other)

★ The Barnacle - in Miami, it is home to Miami pioneer and conservationist Ralph Middleton Monroe

★ Cross Creek - outside of Gainesville, is the home of Florida author Marjorie Kinnan Rawlings

★ Gamble Mansion - in Bradenton, is the antebellum plantation mansion of Major Robert Gamble

★ Kingsley Plantation - on Ft. George Island, is the home of Zephaniah Kingsley

★ Whitehall - in Palm Beach, is home to railroad builder, developer, and "oil man" Henry Flagler

★ Viscaya - Italian Renaissance villa sitting on Biscayne Bay has 10 acres of formal gardens and a stone barge; winter home of James Deering

# Forts & Battlefields

## A few of Florida's famous...

# Forts

- Fort Barancas
- Fort Pickens
- Fort McRee
- Fort Gadsen
- Fort St. Marks
- Fort Clinch
- Castillo de San Marco
- Fort Caroline
- Fort George Island
- Fort Mantanzas
- Fort King
- Fort Brooke
- Fort DeSoto
- Fort Lauderdale
- Fort Jefferson

## Battlefields

- Marianna Battlefields
- Natural Bridge Battlefield
- Olustee Battlefield
- Withaloochee Battlefield
- Okeechobee Battlefield

Fort Jefferson is a national monument that sits on Garden Key in the Dry Tortugas.

Forts & Battlefields

# Libraries

- STATE LIBRARY OF FLORIDA, **Tallahassee**
- P.K. YONGE LIBRARY OF FLORIDA HISTORY, **Gainesville**
- ST. AUGUSTINE HISTORICAL SOCIETY, **St. Augustine**
- JACKSONVILLE PUBLIC LIBRARY
- ST. AUGUSTINE FREE PUBLIC LIBRARY

**Libraries**

The St. Augustine Free Public Library is the oldest library in the state of Florida.

# Zoos & Attractions

Sea World

Cypress Gardens

John Pennekamp Coral Reef State Park

St. Augustine Alligator Farm and Zoological Park

Marineland

Busch Gardens

Florida Aquarium

Lion Country Safari

Metrozoo

Silver Springs

Caribbean Gardens

Parrot Jungle and Gardens

Everglades Wonder Gardens

Devil's Millhopper State Geological Site

Timucuan Ecological and Historic Preserve

Zoos & Attractions

LION

# Museums

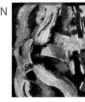

- FLORIDA MUSEUM OF HISPANIC AND LATIN AMERICAN ART, **Coral Gables**
- RINGLING MUSEUM OF ART, **Sarasota**
- FLORIDA MUSEUM OF NATURAL RESOURCES, **Gainesville**

- SALVADOR DALI MUSEUM, **St. Petersburg**
- CONSTITUTION CONVENTION STATE MUSEUM, **Port St. Joe**
- MUSEUM OF FLORIDA HISTORY, **Tallahassee**
- BEAL MALTBIE SHELL MUSEUM, **Winter Park**
- MEL FISHER MARITIME HERITAGE SOCIETY, **The Keys**
- MUSEUM OF ARTS AND SCIENCES, **Miami**
- MARINE LABORATORY AND MUSEUM, **University of Miami**
- U.S. NAVAL AVIATION MUSEUM, **Pensacola**

## MONUMENTS

- Fort Matanzas National Monument
- De Soto National Memorial
- Fort Caroline National Memorial
- Fort Jefferson National Monument
- Castillo de San Marcos National Monument
- Union Monument

## SPACE PLACE!

The John F. Kennedy Space Center is at Cape Canaveral near Cocoa Beach. Cape Canaveral opened as a space research and rocket testing center in 1950. Eight years later, the first American satellite was launched into orbit. In 1961, the first American was launched into space. In 1969, the U.S. landed the first men on the moon.

Monuments & Places

# The Arts

Asolo State Theater, Sarasota
Coconut Grove Playhouse, Miami
Hippodrome Street Theater, Gainesville
Florida Orchestra, St. Petersburg, Tampa, and Clearwater
Performing Arts Center, Miami
Florida Symphony Orchestra, Orlando
Jacksonville Symphony Orchestra, Jacksonville
Philharmonic Orchestra of Florida, Fort Lauderdale
Greater Miami Opera, Miami
Gainesville Civic Ballet, Gainesville
Florida Ballet of Jacksonville, Jacksonville
Southern Ballet Theater of Winter Park, Winter Park
Royal Poinciana Playhouse, Palm Beach

The Arts

The state play is *Cross and Sword*. It is performed through the summer in St. Augustine.

PROPS

## SEASHORES

Canaveral National Seashore has the longest strip of undeveloped shore in the state.

Gulf Islands National Seashore is one of the best beaches of white sand in the state.

## LIGHTHOUSES

Cape Florida Lighthouse is at the end of Key Biscayne. It is Dade County's oldest structure.

The Jupiter Lighthouse in Jupiter was a secret listening post during World War II, called Station "J."

Mt. Dora is proud of its 35-foot (10-meter) mini-lighthouse!

Seashores & Lighthouses

## TRAILS

HAWTHORNE TRAIL, part of Florida's Rails to Trails program. It attracts bicyclers and horseback riders.

PINELLAS TRAIL, hiking and biking city trail of 47 miles (75.2km)

## ROADS

OLD KINGS ROAD, the first graded road built in Florida

DAYTONA BEACH, the only drivable beach in Florida, it was once a beach road where 13 auto speed records were set.

## BRIDGES

SEVEN MILE BRIDGE, part of the 106-mile (169.6 km) Overseas Highway that runs from the mainland to the Keys.

SUNSHINE SKYWAY BRIDGE going over Tampa Bay, opened in 1987; it's 4.1 miles (6.56 kilometers) long

DAME POINT BRIDGE, built in 1989, one of the longest bridges in the world. It crosses the St. Johns River.

Trails, Roads, Bridges, Canals

## CANALS

MIAMI CANAL

CALOOSAHATCHEE RIVER

NORTH NEW RIVER

HILLSBORO CANAL

WEST PALM BEACH CANAL

ST. LUCIE

INTRACOASTAL WATERWAY

## WETLANDS & SWAMPS

• THE EVERGLADES, also known as the "river of grass."
• THE BIG CYPRESS SWAMP
• OKEFENOKEE SWAMP
• CORKSCREW SWAMP SANCTUARY
• BIG GUM SWAMP
• TATE'S HELL SWAMP

## CAVERNS

FLORIDA CAVERNS STATE PARK

Dry caverns feature impressive formations of stalactites, stalagmites, and rock "waterfalls."

Peacock Springs State Recreation Area has one of the longest underwater cave systems in the continental U.S.

A *spelunker* is a person who goes exploring caves!

QUESTION:
• Which is the stalagmite?
• Which is the stalactite?

Wetlands, Swamps, & Caverns

ANSWER: Stalactites are long, tapering formations hanging from the roof of a cavern, produced by continuous watery deposits containing certain minerals. The mineral-rich water dripping from stalactites often forms conical stalagmites on the floor below.

## ANIMALS OF FLORIDA

*Florida animals include:*

Florida panther
Nine-banded armadillo
Fox squirrel
Manatee
Key deer
Bobcat
Cottontail rabbit
White-tailed deer
Coral snake

Black bear
Gray fox
Raccoon
Opossum
Marsh rabbit
Wild pig
Alligator
Crocodile
Gray squirrel
Water moccasin
(cottonmouth)

"Old Joe" Alligator was 11 feet
(3.3 meters) long and weighed
650 lbs. (292.5 kilograms.)
Folklore claims him to have been
200 years old!

# Take a Walk on the Wild Side

Florida has many wildlife preserves and sanctuaries to aid in the survival of endangered animals. The state has spent over $700 million on lands for protecting wildlife.

JAY NORWOOD "DING" DARLING NATIONAL WILDLIFE REFUGE

LAKE WOODRUFF NATIONAL WILDLIFE REFUGE

MERRITT ISLAND NATIONAL WILDLIFE REFUGE

ST. MARKS NATIONAL WILDLIFE REFUGE

ARTHUR B. MARSHALL LOXAHATCHEE NATIONAL WILDLIFE REFUGE

JOHN PENNEKAMP CORAL REEF STATE PARK

(The nation's first underwater preserve protects part of the only living coral reef in North America.)

The country's first National Wildlife Refuge was Pelican Island, established in 1903. Hundreds of species of plants and animals live here.

Gatorade was created in Florida and was named after the University of Florida Gators.

Wildlife Watch

79

# Birds

Birds

**YOU MAY SPY THESE BIRDS!**

Wood Duck

Mourning dove
Mockingbird
Florida jay
Roesate spoonbill
White-crowned pigeon
Anhinga (water turkey)
Mangrove cuckoo
Bobwhite quail
Sparrow
Egret
Heron
Pelican
Vireo
Warbler
Hawk
Ducks
Geese
Turkey

Mourning
Dove

Tern

Thrush

Wren

Flamingo

A hummingbird's wings beat 75 times a second- so fast that you can only see a blur! They make short squeaky sounds, but do not sing.

Ruffed Grouse

## Don't let these Florida bugs bug you!

Brown recluse
Widow spiders
Africanized bees
Chiggers
Fire ants
Fleas
Fruit flies
Mosquitoes
Roaches
Termites
Ticks
Love bugs

Bumblebee

Ants

Butterfly

Praying Mantis

Ladybug

Grasshopper

Do we know any of these bugs?

Maybe... Hey, that ladybug is cute!

The name "love bug" comes from the way they fly in tandem, which means together.

Insects

# Fish

Barracuda
Sailfish
Tarpon
Bonefish
Pompano
Black Mullet
Red Snapper
Menhaden
Marlin
Wahoo
Weakfish
Amberjack
Sea Bass
Speckled Perch
Bream
Bluegill

Fish

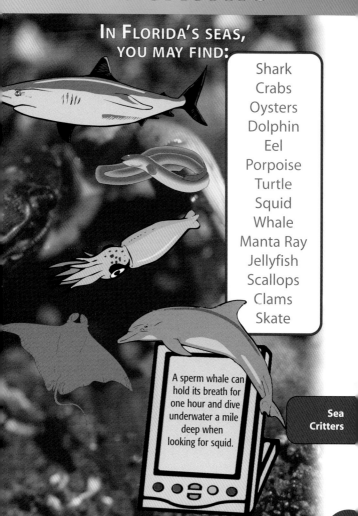

# Sea Critters

## IN FLORIDA'S SEAS, YOU MAY FIND:

Shark
Crabs
Oysters
Dolphin
Eel
Porpoise
Turtle
Squid
Whale
Manta Ray
Jellyfish
Scallops
Clams
Skate

A sperm whale can hold its breath for one hour and dive underwater a mile deep when looking for squid.

# Seashells

*She sells seashells by the Florida seashore!*

Shrimp
Crab
Spiny Lobster
Oyster
Scallop
Conch
Coquina

Mussel
Whelk
Cowrie
Moon Shell
Helmet Shell
Worm Shell
Slipper Shell

**The brilliant white sand on the beaches of northwest Florida is 99% pure quartz crystal. It's formed in the Appalachian Mountains, then ground, polished, and bleached on its journey downriver to the Gulf.**

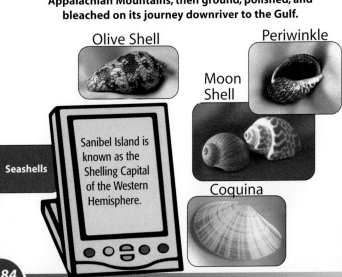

Olive Shell

Periwinkle

Moon Shell

Sanibel Island is known as the Shelling Capital of the Western Hemisphere.

Coquina

**TREEMENDOUS!**

## The "Lone Cypress"

A cypress believed to be two centuries old was once a guide for mariners and fishermen. Efforts to drain swampland and hurricanes stole the lake from the tree. Standing up through a wooden deck, next to the Caloosahatchee Canal and across from the city library in Moore Haven, it continues to stand alone.

**THESE TREES TOWER OVER FLORIDA:**

Slash Pine
Longleaf Pine
Bald Cypress
Southern Red Cedar
Sabal Palm
Water Hickory
Bahama Lysiloma
Florida Fiddlewood
Laurel Oak
Live Oak
Strangler Fig
Sweetbay
Custard Apple
Gumbo-limbo
Red Maple
Red Mangrove
Black Tupelo

Trees

Are you crazy about these Florida wildflowers?

Alligator Lily
Cattail
Bog Buttons
Lizard's Tail
Columbine
Pawpaw
Water Lily
St. John's Wort

Hairy Laurel
Indian Pipes
Wild Azalea
Snowbell
Florida Violet
Sea Rocket
Swamp Mallow
New Jersey Tea
Red Trillium

**Wildflowers**

A red trillium smells like rotten meat! This attracts flies, which pollinate the plant. The roots of this flower were once used to treat rattlesnake bites.

# Cream of the Crops

## Florida's principal agricultural products:

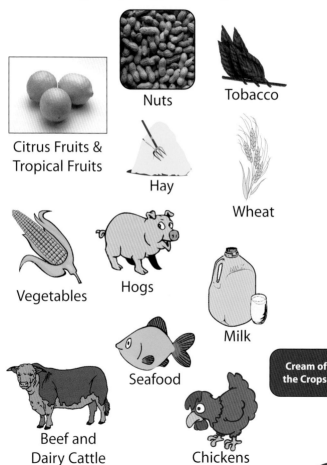

Nuts

Tobacco

Citrus Fruits &
Tropical Fruits

Hay

Wheat

Vegetables

Hogs

Milk

Seafood

Cream of
the Crops

Beef and
Dairy Cattle

Chickens

# First/Big/Small/Etc.

● The world's largest doors–460 feet (14 m)–are found at the Vehicle Assembly Building at Kennedy Space Center.

● One of the world's largest land vehicles is also at the Kennedy Space Center—it's the crawler that brings the shuttles out to the launch pad.

● Key Largo is known as the Dive Capital of the World.

● The first motion picture capital was Jacksonville.

● The first known Christmas in the New World was celebrated by DeSoto and his men in Florida in 1539.

● Lantana has had more reported sightings of UFOs, alien babies, and Elvis Presley than anywhere else in the world. (It's also the home of *The National Enquirer*! )

● The world's deepest and largest freshwater springs are the Wakulla Springs.

● Marineland was the world's first oceanarium.

● Miami installed the first bank automated teller machine especially for rollerbladers.

● The world's smallest police station is a telephone booth in Carabelle.

● America's smallest post office is an 8-foot-by-7-foot shack in Ochopee.

● "The Senator" is the country's largest bald cypress tree. It's more than 3,000 years old.

● Florida has the largest Jewish population in the U.S.

● Miami is the biggest cruise port in the world.

● Venice is the shark tooth capital of the world.

● The *Benwood*, on French Reef in the Keys, is one of the most dived shipwrecks in the world.

● In 1986, one of the world's largest sandcastles was built on Treasure Island. It was five stories tall!

# Festivals

Some Florida Festivals include:

**JANUARY**
*FLORIDA KEYS*
*RENAISSANCE FAIR* -The Keys

**FEBRUARY**
*MIAMI FILM FESTIVAL* - Miami

*SPEEDWEEKS (INLCUDING THE DAYTONA 500)* - Daytona Beach

*OLD ISLAND DAYS* - Key West

*FLORIDA CITRUS FESTIVAL* - Winter Haven

**MARCH**
*BLUEGRASS FESTIVAL* - Kissimmee

**MAY**
*SUNFEST* - West Palm Beach

**JUNE**
*FRIDAY EXTRA CONCERTS* - Tampa

*PENSACOLA SHARK FESTIVAL* - Pensacola

**JULY**
*MICCOSUKEE CRAFTS AND MUSIC FESTIVAL* - Miami

*PEPSI FIRECRACKER 400 AUTO RACE* - Daytona Beach

**AUGUST**
*BOCA FESTIVAL DAYS* - Boca Raton

*DAYS IN SPAIN* - St. Augustine

**SEPTEMBER**
*TAMPA BAY PERFORMING ARTS CENTER* - Tampa

**OCTOBER**
*NATIONAL JAZZ FESTIVAL* - Jacksonville

*BOGGY BAYOU MULLET FESTIVAL* - Niceville

*FLORIDA SEAFOOD FESTIVAL* - Apalachicola

**Festivals**

# Calendar

| | | |
|---|---|---|
| Martin Luther King, Jr. Day *third Monday in January* | Presidents' Day, *3rd Monday in February* | Memorial Day, *last Monday in May* |
| Independence Day, *July 4* | Columbus Day, *2nd Monday in October* | Veterans Day, *November 11* |

## Notes:

State Day (Ponce de León) is April 2.

# Famous Food

## Florida is famous for the following delicious foods!

fried conch
blackened snapper
oysters on the half shell
batter fried catfish
alligator tail
deviled crabs
sushi
seafood gumbo
hushpuppies

key lime pie
grits
fritters
creole jambalaya
steamed jumbo crawfish
paella
moussaka
fried plantains
Native American fry bread

The largest key lime pie was made in Captiva...15 feet (4.5 meters) across! Dessert anyone?

Florida's biggest industry is tourism. That's why most Floridians work in the service industry such as resorts and parks. A lot of business also comes from agriculture, lumber,

fishing, mining, and manufacturing. Oranges are the most important crop in Florida. Many people also work at military bases and the Kennedy Space Center.

Some Floridians have unique jobs such as treasure hunter, trapeze artist, or alligator warden!

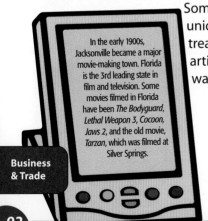

In the early 1900s, Jacksonville became a major movie-making town. Florida is the 3rd leading state in film and television. Some movies filmed in Florida have been *The Bodyguard*, *Lethal Weapon 3*, *Cocoon*, *Jaws 2*, and the old movie, *Tarzan*, which was filmed at Silver Springs.

Business & Trade

# State Books & Websites

*My First Book About Florida* by Carole Marsh
*America the Beautiful: Florida* by Sylvia McNair
*From Sea to Shining Sea: Florida* by Dennis Fradin
*Hello USA: Florida* by Karen Sirvaitis
*Let's Discover the States: Florida* by the Aylesworths
*Portrait of America: Florida* by Kathleen Thompson
*The Florida Experience* by Carole Marsh

## COOL FLORIDA WEBSITES

<u>The Florida Experience!</u>
http://www.floridaexperience.com

<u>Other Florida websites</u>
www.state.fl.us
www.state.fl.us
www.flausa.com
www.50states.com/facts/florida.htm

# Florida
## Glossary

**GLOSSARY WORDS**

**anthropology:** science that deals with physical and cultural development, biological traits, and social customs

**colony:** a territory ruled by a country some distance away

**conservation:** the prevention of decay, waste, or loss

**constitution:** a document outlining the role of a government

**everglade:** a swampy grassland

**Fountain of Youth:** a mythical body of water that supposedly could make old people young again

**immigrant:** a person who moves into a foreign country and settles there

**key:** a low island or reef

**plantation:** a large estate where crops were grown by workers who lived on the estate.

**prosper:** to be successful or fortunate

**ratify:** to approve or confirm

**revolution:** the overthrow of a government

**secede:** to voluntarily give up being a part of an organized group

# Florida
## Spelling Bee

Here are some special Florida-related words to learn! To take the Spelling Bee, have someone call out the words and you spell them aloud or write them on a piece of paper.

**SPELLING WORDS**

| | |
|---|---|
| topography | manatee |
| Tallahassee | Pennekamp |
| mediterranean | anthropologist |
| oceanarium | constitution |
| cypress | coquina |
| Caloosahatchee | artesian |
| Okefenokee | Cape Canaveral |
| sanctuary | Choctawhatchee |
| European | Kissimmee |
| expedition | hurricane |
| stalactites | Apalachicola |
| stalagmites | Wahunsonacock |
| Timucuan | agriculture |

Spelling List

### ABOUT THE AUTHOR...

*CAROLE MARSH has been writing about Florida for more than 20 years. She is the author of the popular Florida State Stuff series for young readers and creator, along with her son, Michael Marsh, of "Florida Facts and Factivities," a CD-ROM widely used in Florida schools. The author of more than 100 Florida books and other supplementary educational materials on the state, Marsh is currently working on a new collection of Florida materials for young people. Marsh correlates her Florida materials to Florida's Sunshine State Standards. Many of her books and other materials have been inspired by or requested by Florida teachers and librarians.*

You know... that was a great experience!

Sure was! Thanks for taking me along.

EDITORIAL ASSISTANT EXTRAORDINAIRE: KARIN PETERSEN